Table of Contents

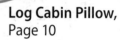

Folded Four-Patch Coasters, Page 2

Log Cabin Pillow, Page 10

Sassy Strip Tote, Page 13

Charming Lap Quilt, Page 26

Introduction

Before you begin your quilting lessons, learn about your sewing machine and practice stitching on scraps of fabric.

Then read through the following general supplies list given below, and quilting how-to tips and quilting vocabulary found in General Instructions, pages 31 and 32. Your lessons will have you turning to these sections for tips.

SUPPLIES YOU WILL NEED

Each lesson will list materials you will need to complete the lesson project. You will also need the basic tools and equipment listed here. Please be careful when handling all the tools and equipment. Some can be dangerous.

- Sewing machine
- Fabric scissors
- Rotary cutter and cutting mat
- Clear quilting ruler
- Straight pins
- Curved quilting safety pins
- Variety of hand-sewing needles
- Seam ripper
- Iron and ironing board
- Water soluble fabric marking pen

i can QUILT

Lesson 1
Folded Four-Patch Coasters

COMPLETING THE COASTER

Stitch right sides together using a ¼" seam allowance unless otherwise indicated.

1. Fold four of the 5" precut squares in half wrong sides together, as shown in Figure 1, and press. Mark with numbers 1–4 and set aside.

Figure 1

2. Position the last 5" precut square right side up on top of the 5" square of batting matching the edges as shown in Figure 2 to make a batting/backing unit.

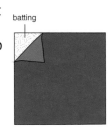

batting

Figure 2

3. Position folded square 1 across the top half of the batting/backing unit matching cut edges (Figure 3). Pin in place.

Figure 3

4. Position folded square 2 on top of the first folded square matching cut edges with the right side of the batting/backing unit as shown in Figure 4. Pin in place.

Figure 4

5. Position folded square 3 across the bottom of the batting/backing unit and on top of folded square 2 as shown in Figure 5 matching cut edges. Pin in place.

Figure 5

6. Remove the pin from folded square 1 and fold un-pinned section back over the upper right corner of folded square 2 as seen in Figure 6a.

a

7. Position folded square 4 on the left side of the batting/ backing unit matching cut edges as seen in Figure 6b.

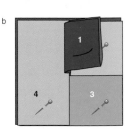

b

8. Unfold folded square 1 to cover the top left corner of folded square 4 as shown in Figure 6c and pin around outside edges to hold.

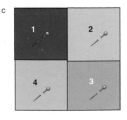

c

Figure 6

9. Stitch ¼" away from all outer edges, pivoting at each corner (Figure 7). Remove all pins.

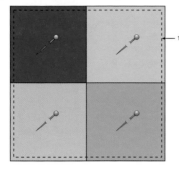

Figure 7

Quilter's Seams

Quilter's want a seam that is the same width the entire length of the seam. Sewing a consistent seam is easy if you take your time and follow these instructions.

• Pin through all layers close to the raw edges.

• Position the raw edges on the ¼" mark on your sewing machine bed under the presser foot and needle.

• Lower the needle into the fabric, lower the presser foot and slowly begin stitching.

• Keep the raw edges moving along the ¼" mark until you have completed the seam.

• Raise the needle and presser foot. Pull the stitched fabric layers away from the needle and clip the threads leaving a thread tail on the seam.

Remember: Practice makes perfect. If you are having problems, practice stitching two or more layers of scrap fabric together.

10. Trim each corner by cutting off some of the seam allowance on the diagonal (Figure 8). Be careful not to cut through the stitching. Trimming the corner will help make sharp, pointed corners after turning right side out.

Figure 8

11. Push the batting/backing to the right side through the folded squares. Carefully push the coaster points out with a pencil or pen. Press coaster flat.

12. Make more coasters by gathering the materials listed for each coaster to be made and repeat all assembly steps. ●

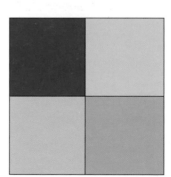

Folded Four-Patch Coasters
Placement Diagram 4½" x 4½"

Lesson 2
Charmed Nine-Patch Treasure Bag

SPECIFICATIONS
7" x 7" folded

WHAT YOU NEED
- 9 coordinating 5" precut squares
- 1 coordinating fat quarter
- 2 (36") pieces of coordinating color ⅛"–¼" cord
- All-purpose thread
- Safety pin
- Basic sewing tools and supplies

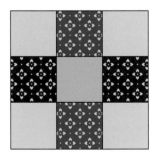

Nine-Patch
14" x 14" Block

CUTTING

1. Cut one 14" square from the coordinating fat quarter.

COMPLETING THE NINE-PATCH BLOCK

1. Arrange the nine 5" precut squares in three rows of three squares each as shown in Figure 1. *Note: You can rearrange the* squares in the rows to make your own color arrangement and design.

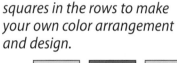

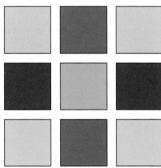

Figure 1

2. Stitch the first row of squares right sides together along one side using a ¼" seam allowance (Figure 2). Press the seam allowances to one side. Go to Pressing on page 31 for tips.

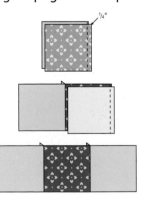

Figure 2

3. Repeat step 2 with the second and third rows. Press the seams in the second row in the opposite direction of row 1 (Figure 3). Press seams in third row in the same direction as row 1 as shown in Figure 3.

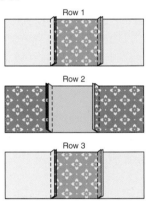

Figure 3

4. Stitch rows right sides together matching seams and long cut edges of rows as shown in Nesting Seams on page 5 to complete the Nine-Patch block shown in Figure 4. Press row seams in one direction. The block should measure 14" on all sides.

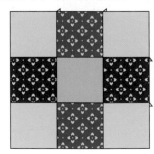

Figure 4

Nesting Seams

It is easier to match seams when sewing rows together in quilting when you "nest" the seams.

• Press the seams in different directions between rows. Go to Pressing on page 31 for tips.

• Begin matching and pinning the edges of the rows together.

• When you come to a seam, position the top seam against the bottom seam with the seam allowances going in opposite directions as shown in Figure A.

Figure A

• Place a pin through the seams to hold in place.

• Continue matching and pinning the edges and stitch.

COMPLETING THE TREASURE BAG

1. Position the Nine-Patch block right sides together on top of the 14" square matching the outside edges and pin (Figure 5).

Figure 5

2. Start in the middle of one side and stitch around all the outer edges using a ¼" seam allowance, pivoting at corners. Stop stitching 4" from where you began, leaving an opening in the seam for turning right side out as shown in Figure 6.

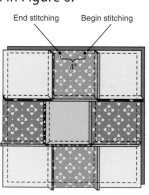

End stitching   Begin stitching

Figure 6

3. Trim each corner by cutting off some of the seam allowance on the diagonal (Figure 7). Be careful not to cut through the stitching. Trimming the corner will help make sharp, pointed corners after turning right side out.

Figure 7

4. Turn the stitched pieces right side out through the seam opening. Carefully push the points out with a pencil or pen.

5. Turn the opening seam allowances to the inside of the stitched pieces and press outside edges flat.

6. Stitch the seam opening closed with matching thread by hand using a slipstitch as seen in Figure 8.

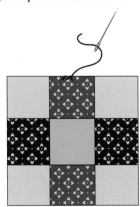

Figure 8

7. With the Nine-Patch block side up, fold a corner of the block in half diagonally to meet the opposite seam lines making a triangle and pin as shown in Figure 9.

Figure 9

8. Repeat with all four corners so that the Nine-Patch block looks like Figure 10.

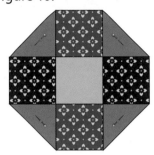

Figure 10

9. Using a water-soluble marker and ruler, draw a stitching line ½" away from a corner fold as seen in Figure 11. Stitch across the triangle corner on the drawn line. Repeat on all four corners.

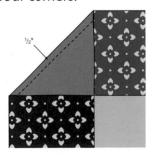

½"

Figure 11

10. Attach a safety pin to one end of one of the cord pieces. Thread the safety pin and cord through the corner seams, beginning with the lower right corner and leaving a tail at the beginning (Figure 12).

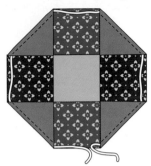

Figure 12

11. Repeat with the second cord beginning with the upper left corner.

12. Tie the ends of each cord together in a knot. Because the cords are threaded in opposite directions, when pulled the cords gather the bag closed. ●

Charmed Nine-Patch Treasure Bag
Placement Diagram 7" x 7"

Lesson 3
Quilted Photo Frame

SPECIFICATIONS
8½" x 10½" (holds 5" x 7" photo)

WHAT YOU NEED
- 2 coordinating fat quarter prints
- 1 (5") precut square coordinating solid or tonal
- #8 coordinating pearl cotton thread
- Batting 9" x 12" rectangle
- Neutral-color all-purpose thread
- 12–16 assorted round or shaped ¼"–1" buttons (optional)
- Hanger (optional)
- Basic sewing tools and supplies

CUTTING

Cut all pieces along the 22" width of the coordinating fat quarter prints. Go to Measuring & Cutting on page 31 for tips.

1. From one of the coordinating fat quarter prints, cut three 2½" x 21" strips for binding.

2. Cut three 2" x 21" strips from the same fat quarter print. Cut the strips into two 2" x 5½" rectangles for C and D, two 2" x 10½" rectangles for E and F, and two 2½" x 6" G strips.

3. From the second coordinating fat quarter print, cut one each 5½" x 7½" B rectangle and 9" x 12" H backing rectangle.

4. From the coordinating square, cut four 2" A squares.

COMPLETING THE PHOTO FRAME TOP

Stitch right sides together using a ¼" seam allowance unless otherwise indicated.

1. Fold each A square in half diagonally wrong sides together to make four A triangles (Figure 1).

Figure 1

2. Pin one A to each corner of B matching the raw edges (Figure 2). Stitch along raw edges using a ⅛" seam allowance as shown in Figure 2 to make the center unit.

Figure 2

3. Stitch C to the top and D to the bottom of the center unit as shown in Figure 3. Press seams toward C and D.

Figure 3

4. Stitch E and F to opposite sides of the center unit as shown in Figure 4. Press seams toward E and F to complete the photo frame top.

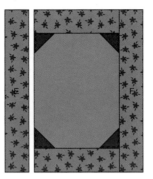

Figure 4

COMPLETING THE HANGING LOOPS

1. To make two loops for hanging the photo frame, fold the G strips in half lengthwise wrong sides together and press (Figure 5a).

Figure 5

2. Open G strips flat and fold long raw edges to the center (Figure 5b); pressing again.

3. Refold and press G strips along the center so that the raw edges are in the center of G as shown in Figure 5c.

4. Stitch close to the open folded side of the G strips (Figure 6). Set aside.

Figure 6

COMPLETING THE PHOTO FRAME

1. Make a quilt sandwich by layering backing H, wrong side up, the batting and centering the photo frame top on top. Pin-baste the layers together. Go to Making a Quilt Sandwich on page 31 for tips.

2. Stitch-in-the-ditch around B using a matching thread color as shown by the white stitching line in Figure 7. Go to Quilting Stitches on page 31 for instructions on stitching-in-the-ditch.

Figure 7

3. Carefully trim the batting and backing H even with the photo frame top edges.

4. Measure and mark backing H side of quilted photo frame 2" from the sides of the top edge.

5. Fold the two G strips in half and pin in place on the H side of the photo frame at the 2" marks, matching raw edges, as shown in Figure 8a.

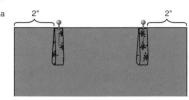
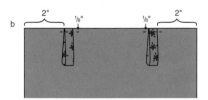

Figure 8

6. Stitch G strips in place using a ⅛" seam allowance (Figure 8b).

7. Go to Binding a Quilt on page 32 for tips to prepare and add binding to complete the photo frame. ●

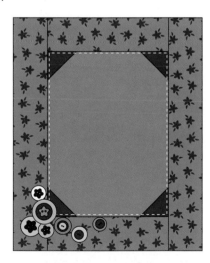

Quilted Photo Frame
Placement Diagram 8½" x 10½"

Try This!

For a bit of glitz, stitch buttons on the photo frame using matching or coordinating colored #8 pearl cotton thread. You can stack the buttons or add one at a time.

1. Thread an embroidery needle with an 18" length of #8 pearl cotton thread. **Do not knot the end.**

2. Stitch through one hole of the button(s) from the front of photo frame to the back, leaving a 4" tail.

Figure 1

3. Stitch back to the front through the other hole of the button(s). *Note: Your stitch on the back should be no wider than the holes of the buttons to be used.*

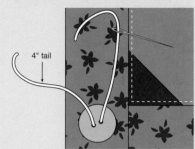

4" tail

Figure 2

4. Trim the pearl cotton leaving at least a 4" tail on each end.

5. Tie the two threads in a square knot to secure the buttons and trim tails to 1" to finish.

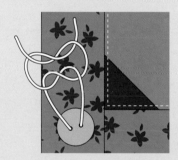

Figure 3

Lesson 4
Log Cabin Pillow

SPECIFICATIONS
Pillow: 17" x 17"

WHAT YOU NEED
- 3 coordinating fat quarters
- 4 (2½" by fabric width) precut coordinating strips
- 16" x 16" pillow form
- Neutral-color all-purpose thread
- Basic sewing tools and supplies

Before You Begin

Checking the Placement Diagram, lay out your fabrics in an arrangement that pleases you before cutting!

Choose a fat quarter for the center area (A) and place right side up on a flat surface. Lay the 2½"-wide strips on top of the fat quarter leaving a square in the middle. Fold each strip in an L-shape to cover two sides of the center area resembling the Placement Diagram.

Make a colored drawing of your arrangement and label the center A area and strips like Figure 8 on page 12 in this pattern.

CUTTING

Go to Measuring & Cutting on page 31 for tips.

1. From one of the coordinating fat quarters, cut one 9½" A square.

2. Cut one 17½" x 20" rectangle from each remaining fat quarter. Label one B and one C.

3. From one 2½" precut strip, cut one 2½" x 9½" No. 1 strip and one 2½" x 11½" No. 2 strip.

4. From a second 2½" precut strip, cut one 2½" x 11½" No. 3 strip and one 2½" x 13½" No. 4 strip.

5. From a third 2½" precut strip, cut one 2½" x 13½" No. 5 strip and one 2½" x 15½" No. 6 strip.

6. From a fourth 2½" precut strip, cut one 2½" x 15½" No. 7 strip and one 2½" x 17½" No. 8 strip.

MAKING A LOG CABIN BLOCK PILLOW FRONT

Stitch right sides together using a ¼" seam allowance unless otherwise indicated.

1. Stitch strip No. 1 to left side of A (Figure 1). Press seam allowance toward strip No. 1.

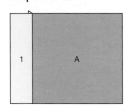

Figure 1

2. Stitch strip No. 2 to the top of A as shown in Figure 2. Press seam allowance toward strip No. 2.

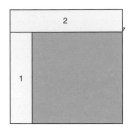

Figure 2

3. Stitch strip No. 3 to the right side of A (Figure 3). Press seam allowance toward strip No. 3.

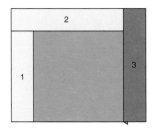

Figure 3

4. Stitch strip No. 4 to the bottom of A as shown in Figure 4. Press seam allowance toward strip No. 4.

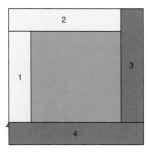

Figure 4

5. Stitch strip No. 5 to the left side of the Log Cabin unit as shown in Figure 5. Press seam allowance toward strip No. 5.

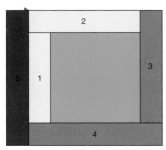

Figure 5

6. Stitch strip No. 6 to the top of the Log Cabin unit (Figure 6). Press seam allowance toward strip No. 6.

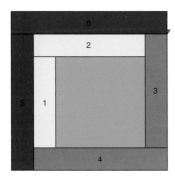

Figure 6

7. Stitch strip No. 7 to the right side of the Log Cabin unit (Figure 7). Press seam allowance toward strip No. 7.

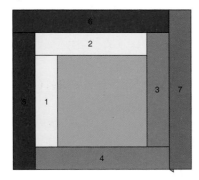

Figure 7

8. Stitch strip No. 8 to the bottom of the Log Cabin unit (Figure 8). Press seam allowance toward strip

No. 8 to complete the Log Cabin block pillow front.

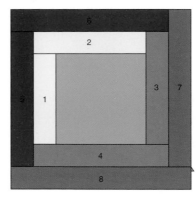

Figure 8

COMPLETING THE PILLOW

1. Fold B and C in half wrong sides together into 10" x 17½" rectangles (Figure 9) and press.

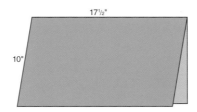

17½"

10"

Figure 9

2. Lay the Log Cabin block pillow front right side up on a flat surface.

3. Position B on top of the Log Cabin block pillow front with the raw edges aligned at the top and the folded edge toward the center as shown in Figure 10. Pin into place.

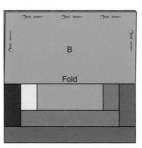

B

Fold

Figure 10

4. Position C on top of the Log Cabin block pillow front with the raw edges aligned at the bottom and the folded edge toward the center as shown in Figure 11. Pin into place.

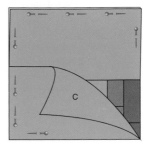

C

Figure 11

5. Stitch around all outer edges and trim corners referring to Figure 12. Turn right side out through the B/C overlap and press edges flat.

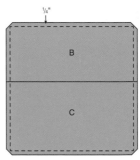

¼"

B

C

Figure 12

6. Topstitch ¼" from outer edges. Insert 16" square pillow form to complete pillow. ●

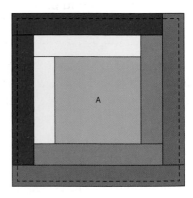

A

Log Cabin Pillow
Placement Diagram 17" x 17"

Lesson 5
Sassy Strip Tote

SPECIFICATIONS
9½" x 3½" x 13"

WHAT YOU NEED
- 8 (2½" by fabric width) coordinating precut strips
- ½ yard coordinating print or solid
- ½ yard muslin
- 2 (1" x 18") pieces nylon strapping
- Batting 14½" x 30"
- Neutral-color all-purpose thread
- 2 (1" x 18") pieces nylon strap
- Blue painter's tape
- Basic sewing tools and supplies

CUTTING

1. Cut seven 2½" x 30" strips from the 2½" precut strips. Set aside the remaining precut strip for binding.

2. Cut one 14½" by fabric width strip from coordinating print or solid. Subcut strip into one 14½" x 30" rectangle for bag lining.

3. Cut one 14½" by fabric width strip from muslin. Subcut strip into one 14½" x 30" rectangle for quilting backing.

COMPLETING THE OUTER BAG

Stitch right sides together using a ¼" seam allowance unless otherwise indicated.

1. Stitch two 2½" x 30" strips together on the long sides (Figure 1a). Continue stitching strips to the first two along the long sides until all seven strips have been stitched together as shown in Figure 1b. Press all seams in the same direction. **Note:** *This is commonly referred to as strip piecing. It is a quick and accurate way to stitch evenly sized lengths of fabric together to be cut into units to make blocks or to create a striped fabric for a bag!*

Figure 1

2. Tape the muslin rectangle to a flat surface with blue painter's tape on all four corners.

3. Center batting on muslin and strip-pieced outer bag on batting right side up to make a layered quilt sandwich (Figure 2). Make sure all sandwich layers are smooth.

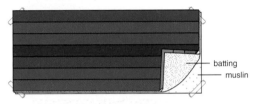

batting
muslin

Figure 2

4. Use quilter's bent safety pins to pin-baste layers together positioning pins approximately 3" apart all over the quilt sandwich.

5. Quilt the sandwiched layers as desired. Go to Quilting Stitches on page 31 for tips. The sample bag was quilted using a meandering pattern.

SQUARING BAG CORNERS

1. Fold the quilted and pieced outer bag in half right sides together along the length. Pin and stitch both sides (Figure 3). Press seams open.

fold

Figure 3

2. To square both bottom corners, match the side seams to the fold on the bag bottom at each corner. Measure and mark a stitching line 3" from the corner points as shown in Figure 4a.

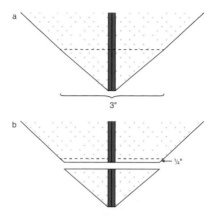

Figure 4

3. Stitch on the marked lines and trim the seam allowances to ¼" as shown in Figure 4b. Turn bag right side out.

4. Fold the 14½" x 30" lining rectangle in half right sides together to measure 14½" x 15". Pin and stitch sides.

5. Repeat steps 2 and 3 with both corners of the lining piece. **Do not turn lining right side out.**

COMPLETING THE BAG

1. Place lining inside the quilted strip-pieced outer bag wrong sides together and matching the side seams and top raw edges. Pin around top raw edges (Figure 5).

Figure 5

2. Measure 3" from each side seam on both the front and back of the outer bag. Position and pin the nylon strips to the top raw edge of the outer bag as shown in Figure 6.

Figure 6

3. Baste ⅛" from the top raw edges securing lining, quilted strip-pieced outer bag and handles.

4. Take the precut strip set aside for binding and fold 1" of one short end to the wrong side. Fold strip in half lengthwise wrong sides together and press.

5. Pin binding strip to top edge of bag, matching raw edges. Stitch to bag starting 1" from folded end using a ¼" seam allowance tucking unfolded end inside folded end before finishing stitching. Go to Binding a Quilt on page 32. ●

Sassy Strip Tote
Placement Diagram 9½" x 3½" x 13"

Lesson 6
Pinwheel Pot Holder

SPECIFICATIONS
8" x 8"

WHAT YOU NEED
- 1 fat quarter print
- 1 fat quarter contrasting solid
- 1 (10" square) needlepunched insulating batting
- Neutral-color all-purpose thread
- Basic sewing tools and supplies

Caution!
Pot holders need to have a layer of needlepunched insulating batting inside to reflect the heat from pots and pans away from your hand. Needlepunched insulating batting also does not melt.

This type of batting has a shiny side that should be placed toward the heat source or the pot holder side you expect to use next to the pots.

You can make the pot holder even more heat resistant by adding one or two layers of a thin cotton batting between the insulated batting and the right side of the pot holder. Just cut the cotton batting the same size as the insulated batting.

Never use polyester batting in pot holders. It melts!

CUTTING
1. Cut two 2½" x 21" D strips from print fat quarter.

2. Cut one 10" x 21" strip from print fat quarter. Subcut one 10" C square and two 4⅞" A squares.

3. Cut one 4⅞" x 18" strip from contrasting solid fat quarter. Subcut two 4⅞" B squares.

COMPLETING THE PINWHEEL BLOCK

Stitch right sides together using a ¼" seam allowance unless otherwise indicated.

1. Draw a diagonal line on the wrong side of each B square as shown in Figure 1.

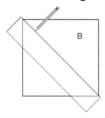
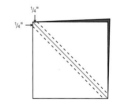

Figure 1   **Figure 2**

2. Position a B square on top of an A square right sides together matching raw edges. Stitch ¼" from line on either side of drawn line (Figure 2).

3. Cut on the drawn line as shown in Figure 3 to make two A-B half-square units. Press the seam open. *Note: Pressing the seams open on a pinwheel block*

reduces the bulk that must be sewn through at the center of the block.

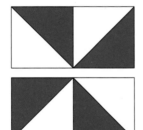

Figure 3

4. Repeat steps 2 and 3 with the remaining A and B squares to make four A-B half-square units.

5. Match the B side of one A-B half-square unit to the A side as shown in Figure 4 and stitch. Press the seam open. Repeat with the remaining A-B units to make two rows as shown again in Figure 4.

Figure 4

6. Stitch the two rows together matching the seams and raw edges to complete a Pinwheel block for the pot holder right side (Figure 5).

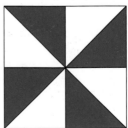

Figure 5

COMPLETING THE POT HOLDER

1. Lay the C square right side down and center the thermal batting, shiny side down, on top. Layer the pinwheel block right side up and centered on the batting as shown in Figure 6. Pin-baste to hold, making a quilt sandwich.

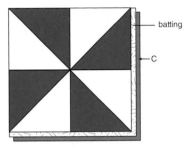

Figure 6

2. Quilt the sandwiched block as desired. Go to Quilting Stitches on page 31 for tips. The sample project was quilted using a meandering pattern.

3. Trim all outside edges even with the pinwheel block.

4. Stitch the D strips together on the short ends; press seam to one side. Press D in half lengthwise wrong sides together to prepare a binding strip.

5. Starting at one corner, stitch D to the pinwheel side of the quilted pot holder. Go to Binding a Quilt on page 32 for tips on how to miter the first three corners as shown in Figure 7.

6. At the fourth corner, continue to stitch straight and overlap the binding beginning, leaving a tail as shown again in Figure 7. Trim the tail to 5" long.

7. Turn the binding to the back of the pot holder and hand-stitch in place to the end of the 5" tail using a slipstitch as shown in Figure 8.

8. Fold the 5" tail in half, overlapping onto the pot holder back and stitch in place by hand or machine to make a hanging loop (Figure 9). ●

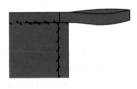

Figure 9

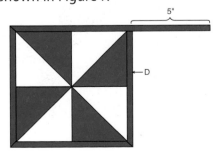

5"

D

Figure 7

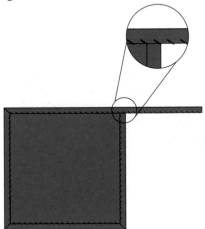

Figure 8

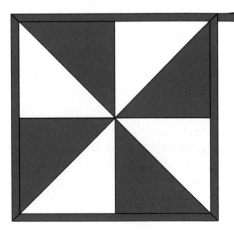

Pinwheel Pot Holder
Placement Diagram 8" x 8"

i can QUILT

Lesson 7
Comfort Muscle Wrap

SPECIFICATIONS
6½" x 17"

WHAT YOU NEED
- 1 fat quarter flannel
- 12 (5") precut coordinating squares
- Flaxseed (3–5 cups)
- Neutral-color all-purpose thread
- Basic sewing tools and supplies

CUTTING

1. Cut one 12½" x 18" rectangle from flannel.

COMPLETING THE WRAP COVER

Stitch right sides together using a ¼" seam allowance unless otherwise indicated.

1. Arrange the 12 (5") precut squares into four rows of three squares as shown in Figure 1. *Note: Move the squares around until you like the way they look!*

Figure 1

2. Stitch the squares in the first row together (Figure 2). Repeat with the squares in each row to make four rows. Press seams in opposite directions between rows. Go to Pressing on page 31 for tips.

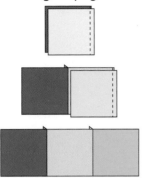

Figure 2

3. Stitch the rows together, matching raw edges and seams as shown in Figure 3, to make a pieced unit. Go to Nesting Seams on page 5 for tips. Press seams in one direction.

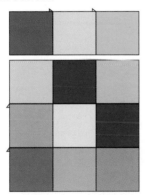

Figure 3

4. Fold the pieced unit in half right sides together to have a rectangle 7½" x 18½" as shown in Figure 4.

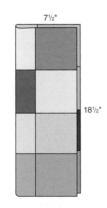

7½"

18½"

Figure 4

5. Stitch together the long sides and one short side of the pieced unit and trim corner (Figure 5). Turn right side out.

Figure 5

6. On the unstitched short end, fold and press the raw edge toward the wrong side of the fabric ¼" as shown in Figure 6a.

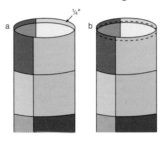

¼"

a   b

Figure 6

7. Fold and press ¼" to the wrong side again. Pin and stitch in place along the first fold as shown in Figure 6b making a double-turned ¼" hem to complete the wrap cover.

COMPLETING THE MUSCLE WRAP

1. Fold the 12½" x 18" flannel rectangle in half right sides together to have a rectangle 6¼" x 18". Stitch together the one long and one short side of the rectangle (Figure 7). Trim corner and turn right side out.

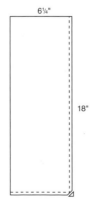

6¼"

18"

Figure 7

2. On the unstitched short end, fold and press ¼" of the raw edge toward the wrong side of the fabric (Figure 8). Fill the flannel sack half full with flaxseed.

¼"

Figure 8

3. Pin the unstitched short end closed matching pressed edges (Figure 9). Stitch closed through all layers close to the fold.

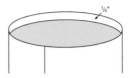

Figure 9

4. Insert completed muscle wrap into wrap cover.

TO USE

For a heat wrap, place the Comfort Muscle Wrap in the microwave for 1–2 minutes on high or until warm to the touch, or store the wrap in the freezer for a cold compress. ●

Comfort Muscle Wrap
Placement Diagram 6½" x 17"

Lesson 8
Chalkboard Place Mat

SPECIFICATIONS
14" x 18½"

WHAT YOU NEED
- 3 fat quarters matching print
- ½ yard chalkboard fabric
- Batting 16" x 20"
- Neutral-color all-purpose thread
- ⅛"-wide basting tape (optional)
- Fabric basting spray (optional)
- Basic sewing tools and supplies

CUTTING

1. Set aside one fat quarter for the place mat back.

2. Cut eight 2½" x 21" strips from two fat quarters. Set aside four 2½" x 21" strips for binding.

3. Subcut four of the 2½" x 21" strips into one 2½" x 10½" B strip, one 2½" x 17½" A strip and two 2½" x 19" C strips.

Caution!
Pinning chalkboard fabric will leave holes in the fabric, so pin close to the raw edges or position ⅛" basting tape on the edges of the chalkboard rectangle. Remove the protective paper and position the A, B and C strips right sides together and matching the raw edges. Stitch together.

4. Cut one 10½" x 14½" rectangle chalkboard fabric.

COMPLETING THE PLACE MAT

Stitch right sides together using a ¼" seam allowance unless otherwise indicated.

1. Place a pin 8" from the right short end of the A strip. Fold A right sides together at the pin as shown in Figure 1a.

2. Place a pin 3½" away from the fold as shown in Figure 1b. Fold the top strip end back to the right at the pin to make a strip 10½" long as shown in Figure 1c.

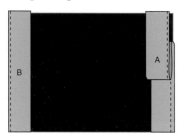

Figure 1

3. Pin through all layers at the folds to hold and press the folds in place with an iron.

4. Position the folded A strip on the right side of the chalkboard rectangle with right sides together and matching raw edges (Figure 2).

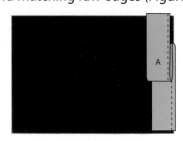

Figure 2

Pin in place, placing the pins close to the raw edge and stitch together.

5. Stitch strip B in the same manner to the left side of the rectangle (Figure 3).

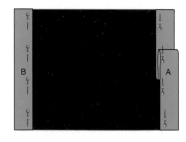

Figure 3

6. Finger-press A and B away from the chalkboard fabric rectangle and pin in place on the fabric side of the seam through all seam allowances as shown in Figure 4. Go to No Ironing? Finger-Press Instead on page 22.

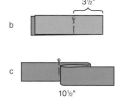

Figure 4

7. Stitch a C strip to the top and the bottom of the chalkboard rectangle in the same manner as A and B. Finger-press the seams and pin as

in step 6 and as shown in Figure 5 to complete the place mat top.

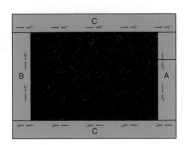

Figure 5

No Pins? Spray!

For small projects or where pinning might be harmful to the project, use a fabric basting spray to hold the quilt sandwich layers together.

• Spray the wrong side of the quilt back with the basting spray. ***Note:*** *Be sure to have an old sheet underneath your* *project to catch the extra spray around your project.*

• Center and smooth the batting over the backing.

• Spray the batting and then smooth the quilt top wrong side down over the batting.

Fabric basting spray will hold your project together while you stitch.

8. Make a quilt sandwich by positioning the place mat back fat quarter right side down and centering the batting on top.

9. Center the place mat top on the batting. Pin around the outside edges through all layers to hold in place being careful to not pin in the chalkboard rectangle.

10. Topstitch around the chalkboard fabric close to the A, B and C seams as seen in Figure 6 to secure the layers.

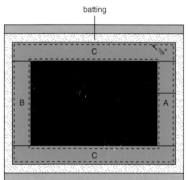

Figure 6

11. Stitch again ⅜" from the outside edges of the place mat top as shown in Figure 6. Trim the batting and back layers even with the place mat top edges.

12. Make and apply binding using the four 2½" x 21" binding strips set aside following instructions in Binding a Quilt on page 32 to complete the place mat. ●

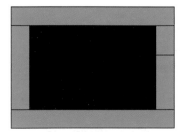

Chalkboard Place Mat
Placement Diagram 14" x 18½"

No Ironing? Finger-Press Instead

Chalkboard fabric will melt. **Do not iron this project.** Instead finger-press seams.

Stitch seams as instructed. Then push the upper fabric away from the bottom fabric with your fingers (Figure 1).

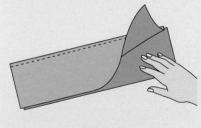

Figure 1

Gently hold the upper fabric in place while running your fingers along the seam line (Figure 2). Do this several times until the seam lays flat.

Figure 2

Use finger pressing any time you cannot use an iron or when stitching small pieces together.

Lesson 9
Pretty Pouch

SPECIFICATIONS
4" x 4½" (excluding strap)

WHAT YOU NEED
- 1 fat quarter
- 1 yard ½"-wide coordinating ribbon
- 1 (1") piece hook-and-loop fastener
- Buttons
- #8 pearl cotton thread
- Neutral-color all-purpose thread
- Basic sewing tools and supplies

CUTTING

1. Fold the fat quarter in half right sides together. Using the full-size pattern included on pages 24 and 25, position the pattern on the folded fat quarter and pin to hold.

2. Cut out the pattern along the solid outer line to cut two Pretty Pouch pieces. Use chalk or a water-soluble marking tool to copy all pattern marks to both fabric pieces. Go to Measuring & Cutting on page 31 for tips.

COMPLETING THE POUCH

Stitch right sides together using a ¼" seam allowance unless otherwise indicated.

1. Position the ends of the ribbon at the squares on the right side of one Pretty Pouch piece matching

the ribbon ends to fabric edges as shown in Figure 1. Baste ⅛" from fabric edge to secure in place.

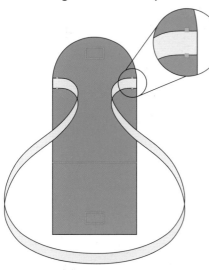

Figure 1

2. Position Pretty Pouch pieces right sides together matching all edges. Tuck the ribbon between the pieces away from the edges and pin together.

3. Stitch around the edges, leaving a 3" opening along one long side as shown in Figure 2.

4. Turn the Pretty Pouch right side out, gently pushing out square corners. Turn opening seam allowance to inside and press edges flat. Slipstitch opening closed (Figure 3).

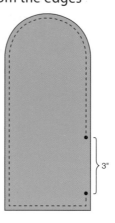

3"

Figure 2

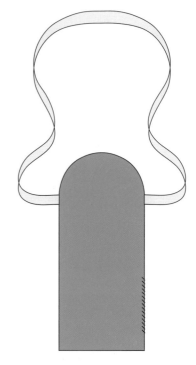

Figure 3

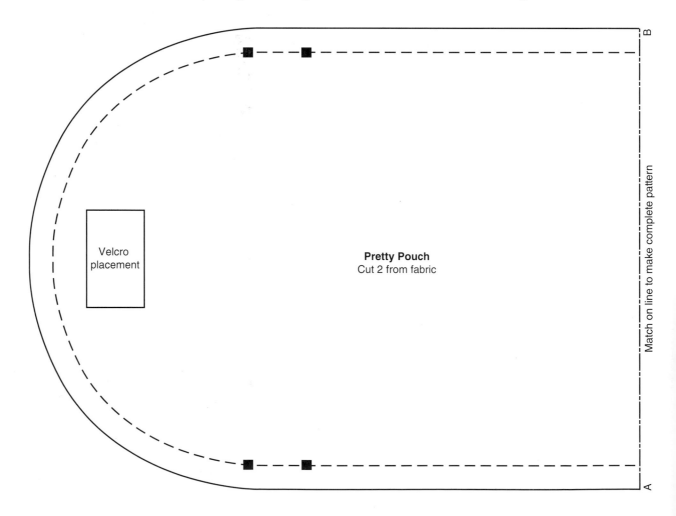

Velcro placement

Pretty Pouch
Cut 2 from fabric

B

Match on line to make complete pattern

A

5. Position and stitch the loop side of the hook-and-loop fastener on the straight bottom edge of the Pretty Pouch where marked (Figure 4).

6. Turn the Pretty Pouch over and add the hook side of the hook-and-loop fastener at the top of the curved edge as marked and shown in Figure 4.

7. Fold the straight bottom edge up toward the curved edge along the marked fold line and pin in place as shown in Figure 5.

8. Topstitch ¼" from the edges as shown in Figure 6. Do not stitch across the bottom folded edge. Fold curved edge down connecting the hook-and-loop fastener to create pouch flap.

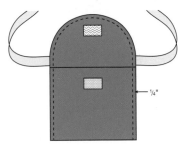

Figure 6

9. Add buttons to pouch flap following the "Try This!" button instructions given in Lesson 3 on page 7, to cover the stitching for the hook-and-loop fastener. ●

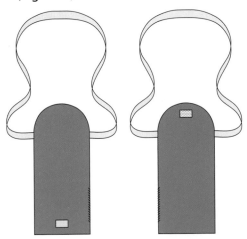

Figure 4

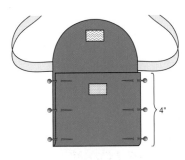

4"

Figure 5

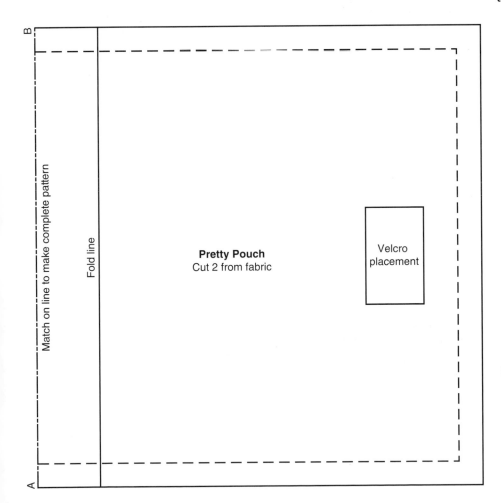

B

Match on line to make complete pattern

Fold line

Pretty Pouch
Cut 2 from fabric

Velcro placement

A

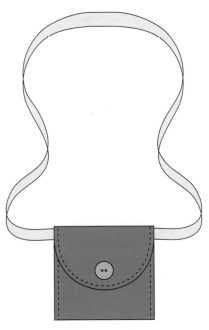

Pretty Pouch
Placement Diagram 4" x 4½" excluding strap

i can QUILT

Lesson 10
Charming Lap Quilt

CUTTING

Go to Measuring & Cutting on page 31 for tips.

1. Cut five 2½" by fabric width solid white strips. Subcut two 2½" x 36" A border strips. Set aside three strips for B borders.

COMPLETING THE QUILT TOP

Stitch right sides together using a ¼" seam allowance unless otherwise indicated.

1. Arrange the 80 (5") precut squares on a large, flat surface in 10 rows of eight squares each as shown in Figure 1. ***Note:*** *Move the squares around until you like the way they look!*

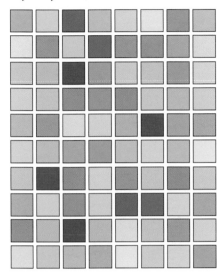

Figure 1

2. Stitch the squares in the first row together as you arranged them (Figure 2). Place the stitched row back in the arrangement.

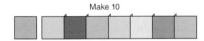

Make 10

Figure 2

3. Repeat, stitching the squares in the next row together. Put the stitched row back in the arrangement. Stitch together all 10 rows. Press the seam allowances in opposite directions between rows. Go to Pressing on page 31 for tips.

4. Pin the first row to the second row right sides together matching edges and nesting seams. Go to Nesting Seams on page 5 for tips. Stitch together and press seam toward the first row.

5. Repeat, adding each row one at a time to complete the quilt top as shown in Figure 3. Press each seam toward the first row after each row is added.

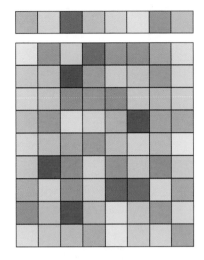

Figure 3

ADDING QUILT BORDERS

1. Stitch an A border to the top of the quilt top. Press the seam toward A. Stitch the second A border to the bottom of the quilt top as seen in Figure 4. Press the seam toward A.

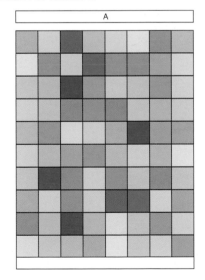

Figure 4

2. Stitch the three border strips set aside earlier together on the short ends to make one long strip. Press the seams in one direction.

3. Cut two 2½" x 49½" B border strips from the long strip.

4. Stitch a B border to each side of the quilt top as shown in Figure 5. Press seams toward B.

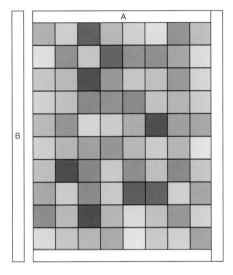

Figure 5

MAKING THE QUILT SANDWICH

Go to Making a Quilt Sandwich on page 31 for tips.

1. Press the backing fabric smooth.

2. Lay the batting out on a large flat surface. Smooth out all wrinkles. Tape the batting corners to the surface with blue painter's tape.

3. Lay the backing fabric right side up and centered on top of the batting. Smooth out wrinkles.

4. Lay the quilt top, right side down and centered, on the backing and batting (Figure 6). Smooth out any wrinkles.

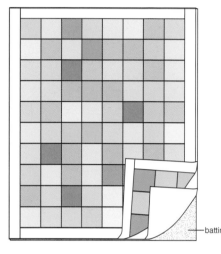

Figure 6

5. Pin the layers together around the quilt top outer edge.

6. Stitch around the quilt sandwich ¼" from the quilt top outer edge. Leave a 10" opening on one long side.

7. Trim the batting and backing fabric even with the quilt top edges. Trim the corners at an angle as shown in Figure 7.

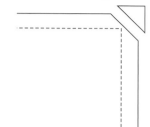

Figure 7

8. Carefully turn the quilt sandwich right sides out through the 10" seam opening. Smooth the layers flat and push the corners out with a pencil or pen. Press the stitched edges flat.

9. Turn the opening edges to the inside ¼". Pin together and press. Slipstitch the opening closed by hand.

10. Topstitch all around the quilt ¼" from the edges.

TYING YOUR QUILT

1. Lay the quilt on a large flat surface and smooth out.

2. Thread a hand needle with an 18" strand of #8 pearl cotton thread. Do not knot the ends.

3. Insert needle from front to back and back up to the front at a seam intersection between the quilt top squares through all layers (Figure 8).

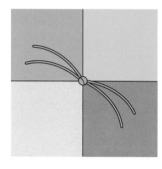

Figure 8

4. Tie a square knot with thread tails as shown in Figure 8. Go to "Try This!" on page 9 for tips on how to tie a square knot.

5. Tie square knots at each corner of all the quilt top squares to finish the quilt. ●

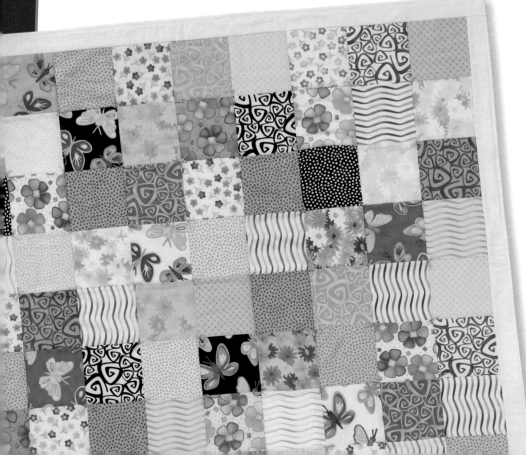

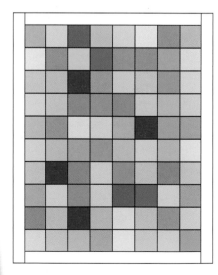

Charming Lap Quilt
Placement Diagram 41" x 49½"

Lesson 11
Pillowcase

SPECIFICATIONS
Standard pillowcase size

WHAT YOU NEED
- ⅛ yard coordinating print or solid fabric 1
- ½ yard coordinating print or solid fabric 2
- 1 yard print or solid fabric 3
- All-purpose, neutral-color thread
- Basic sewing tools and supplies

CUTTING

Go to Measuring & Cutting on page 31 for tips.

1. Cut one 2" by fabric width fabric 1 strip. Subcut one 2" x 42" A strip.

2. Cut one 11" by fabric width fabric 2 strip. Subcut one 11" x 42" B strip.

3. Cut one 27" by fabric width fabric 3 rectangle. Subcut one 27" x 42" C rectangle.

Want to Make a Difference!

Making a pillowcase for a charity can be fun and very rewarding. Check with your local quilt shop for charities that accept them and how to donate.

29

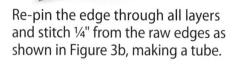

COMPLETING THE PILLOWCASE

Stitch right sides together using a ¼" seam allowance unless otherwise indicated.

1. Press all pieces flat.

2. Fold A in half lengthwise wrong sides together and press.

3. Lay B right side up on a flat surface. Position A on B matching raw edges along the fabric width (Figure 1).

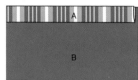

Figure 1

4. Position C right side down on the A and B pieces matching raw edges along the fabric width as shown in Figure 2.

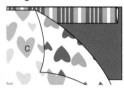

Figure 2

5. Pin the layers together along the width.

6. Beginning at the unpinned edge, roll C up toward the pinned edge as shown in Figure 3a.

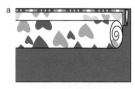

Figure 3

7. Fold the unpinned edge of B up over C to match the pinned edge.

Re-pin the edge through all layers and stitch ¼" from the raw edges as shown in Figure 3b, making a tube.

8. Pull C out one end of the tube. As you pull C out, the tube formed by piece B will turn right side out with the seam allowance between the two B sides (Figure 4). Press A toward B.

Figure 4

9. Fold stitched unit in half wrong sides together to make a rectangle approximately 21" x 31½" as shown in Figure 5. Press.

31½"

21"

Figure 5

10. Use a straight edge and rotary cutter to trim ½" from long side and straighten raw edge across bottom if necessary.

11. Stitch the raw edges together using a ¼" seam allowance. Trim the corner at a diagonal.

12. Turn the pillowcase wrong side out and press seams flat.

13. Stitch ⅜" from the seam to enclose the first seam allowance inside as shown in Figure 6. Press flat and turn right side out. ●

⅜" seam

Figure 6

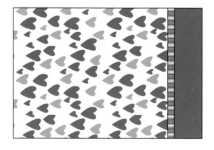

Pillowcase
Placement Diagram Standard Pillowcase Size

General Instructions

QUILTING HOW-TO TIPS

Here are some general tips that will help you understand the techniques introduced in this book. If you have more questions, go to your local library, purchase a quilting guide book or ask an adult quilter.

Measuring & Cutting

When using a rotary cutter and mat, place a fabric edge along one of the grid lines on the mat. Place the ruler at right angles to the fabric edge and make a straight cut to straighten the edge (Figure 1a).

Measure required widths of strips to be cut from the straightened edge using the ruler and the mat grids. Cut strips first and then squares, rectangles or triangles as directed in the cutting instructions (Figure 1b).

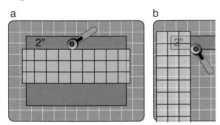

Figure 1

Pressing

Set stitches by pressing seams flat.

Generally, press seam allowances toward the darker fabric.

Press seams in opposite directions row to row (Figure 2). This helps when matching seams and reduces bulk.

Press to avoid bulky areas that will be difficult to stitch through.

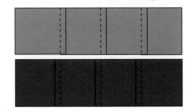

Figure 2

Making a Quilt Sandwich

Layering the quilt top with batting and backing is known as making a quilt sandwich. Iron the backing and place it right side down on a clean, flat surface. For large projects, tape the edges down, keeping it smooth and even.

Place the batting centered on top of the backing, smoothing out the wrinkles (Figure 3).

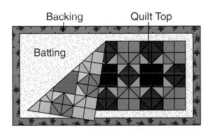

Figure 3

Center the quilt top wrong side down on the batting.

The batting and backing layers will usually be larger than the quilt top.

Baste the layers together to prevent shifting during quilting. Position curved quilting safety pins through all layers every 3–6" all over the quilt top.

Quilting Stitches

The instruction to "quilt as desired" leaves the quilting design up to you. Here are four simple quilting designs that you can begin with. They require no marking of stitching patterns. Practice your quilting on scrap layers of fabric or paper.

Meandering or stippling are allover quilting patterns that are a series of random curved lines that fill the entire area (Figure 4). Stitch-in-the-ditch and outline quilting are stitched following seam lines in the quilt top. Channel quilting is parallel lines of stitching an equal distance apart.

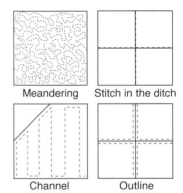

Figure 4

To machine quilt, use a long stitch length (3.0 or 8–10 stitches per inch). Loosen the presser foot pressure. Use a specialty sewing machine foot called an even-feed or walking foot to prevent tucks and puckering in the fabric layers. Your sewing machine manual should give suggestions for quilting with your machine.

Remove the safety pins as you quilt. Never stitch over the pins.

Binding a Quilt

When quilting is done, finish the edges of your quilt with strips of fabric called binding.

1. Join binding strips on short ends with ¼" seam allowances. Press seams open. Fold 1" of one end to wrong side and press. Fold binding strip in half lengthwise wrong sides together and press (Figure 5).

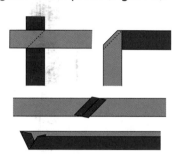

Figure 5

2. Begin to stitch binding to quilt top a short distance from a corner, matching raw edges, using a ¼" seam and leaving the end of binding unstitched. Stop stitching ¼" from corner and backstitch (Figure 6).

Stop ¼"

Figure 6

3. Remove quilt from machine and turn. Fold binding up at a 45-degree angle to seam, and then down even with quilt edges forming a pleat at corner (Figure 7).

Figure 7

4. Resume stitching at corner, backstitching ¼" from second corner. Repeat until reaching starting point (Figure 8).

Stop ¼"

Figure 8

5. Cut binding off long enough to tuck inside starting end and complete stitching (Figure 9).

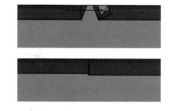

Figure 9

6. Turn binding to quilt back and stitch in place by hand using a slipstitch.

QUILTING VOCABULARY

Basting Basting is done to hold several layers of fabric and batting together. It can be done by pinning the layers together or hand-stitching with long stitches.

Binding The fabric strips that cover the raw edges of a project to finish those edges so they will last longer.

Block This is the basic design part of a quilt. Small pieces are stitched together to form a design like a star or a checkerboard pattern called a Nine-Patch block.

Pieced or Piecing Stitching several small pieces, strips or units of fabric together to make a block or quilt top.

Precuts These are fabrics that you buy already cut to a certain size. The lessons in this book use several precut sizes. Here are their common names and sizes: 5" squares (Charms), 18" x 22" pieces (Fat Quarters) and 2½" by fabric width strips (Jelly Rolls).

Press or Pressing Using an iron to smooth fabric before cutting. Also using an iron to move and secure seams in a certain direction.

Seam Allowance This is the measurement from the raw edges of the fabric to where the sewing machine needle enters the fabric. Quilters use a ¼" seam allowance.

Slipstitch A hand-stitch used to close an opening or to sew down the binding to the back of the quilt.

Subcutting Cutting a larger piece of fabric into smaller pieces. For example: Cutting a 5" by fabric width strip into 5" squares.

Topstitching Stitch the distance given from the edge of the project through all layers to secure the edges.

Quilting The hand or machine stitching used to hold together the layers of a quilt or quilted project. This can also mean the steps taken to make a quilt or quilted project. ●

Annie's™ *I Can Quilt* is published by Annie's, 306 East Parr Road, Berne, IN 46711. Printed in USA. Copyright © 2012 Annie's.

ISBN: 978-1-59217-460-7

1 2 3 4 5 6 7 8 9